MUSIC
in Medieval Manuscripts

NICOLAS BELL

THE BRITISH LIBRARY

omme ne m
furoze tuoar
gua me neqz
m ria tua coz

INTRODUCTION

Music formed an intrinsic part of cultural life throughout the Middle Ages. Its position was quite different from that which music has held in later times, and in many respects was more integrated into the ways of life which developed through the medieval period. Our knowledge of medieval musical life comes from a very wide range of different documents, but almost all the surviving sources are connected in some way with the church. This is not to say that there was no tradition of secular music-making, but it demonstrates the powerful control which the church exercised over culture, especially over the literate culture which came to be preserved in medieval manuscripts. Our knowledge of folk traditions and secular music-making, especially in the early Middle Ages, is generally slight and circumstantial, though nevertheless significant.

Most of the music illustrated in this book was written down for use in worship within the Christian liturgy. It is impossible to understand medieval music in isolation from the situations in which it was used. Plainchant, the unmeasured and generally unaccompanied music setting the texts of the mass and of the various other daily services collectively known as the office, was always sung within specific contexts. Its primary purpose was to convey the meaning of the words, but even this fusion of music and words provides only one element which, combined with the ritual, the architecture and decorations, and the time and season, together make up the spiritual experience of worship.

The main function of this music, then, is not to serve as an end in itself, but to help articulate the words which it sets. This could be done either by simply enhancing the natural rhythm and phrasing of the spoken word, or by adding solemnity and grandeur with long 'melismas', or streams of notes sung to a single syllable, a practice which St Augustine of Hippo, writing around 400 AD, saw as a direct expression by the human soul of a joy too deep for words.

Almost all the music that was written down in the medieval period was vocal music, and in most cases it was intended to be performed by voices alone, without instruments. Furthermore, apart from whistles and other 'functional' instruments, very few musical instruments survive from before the very end of the Middle Ages, in the late fifteenth century. Much of our knowledge of medieval music-making outside the context of the liturgy, and particularly of instrumental music, derives again from manuscripts, in this case not from the notated texts themselves, but from the illuminations which surround them. In some cases the artists of these illuminations do not depict instruments in current usage so much as their ideas of how instruments from Biblical times may have looked. An example is the full-page illustration from the Vespasian Psalter, one of the most beautifully illuminated manuscripts

of the eighth century, possibly from Canterbury, which shows King David with his lyre, surrounded by trumpeters, percussion players and dancers. But in other cases it is a testimony to the inseparable bonds between church and society that illustrations of secular musicians and instruments are found illuminating not only religious texts, but also books intended for use in the liturgy, such as the musicians from the margins of the Breviary of Renaud de Bar (Yates Thompson MS 8, f.53, *below*).

The British Library houses an exceptionally broad range of musical sources, with examples of virtually every type of music writing from the very earliest times onwards, as well as many thousands of medieval illustrations of music-making. Together these form a collection of immense historical value, and this book can do no more than present a small but representative selection of examples, in the hope of demonstrating something of the rich variety in the musical culture of the Middle Ages.

UNDERSTANDING MUSIC

Throughout the Middle Ages, it was generally believed in western Europe that Gregorian chant was a divine music which had been dictated to St Gregory the Great by the Holy Spirit in the form of a dove. St Gregory is often depicted with a dove singing in his ear, writing down the music which he hears, as in this eleventh-century manuscript. Modern research suggests that this picture should not be taken entirely literally, and that the role actually played by Gregory, who was Pope from 590 to 604, was more one of attempting to unify the wide range of different liturgical chant practices which had arisen in the preceding centuries. This was one component of the substantial church reforms which took place under his papacy. In addition to the firm evidence of a multitude of different chant traditions, both before and after Gregory's time, there is another problem with the medieval understanding of Gregory copying down the divine chant: no musical notation survives from before the ninth century, and so the picture of Gregory writing down music at the end of the sixth century is impossible to substantiate. For most of the first millennium of Christianity, our evidence shows that chant must have been passed down not by writing, but by an oral tradition.

The Holy Spirit dictates chant to St Gregory. Harley MS 3011, f. 69v.

7

Despite the lack of musical sources, we do know something about how music was understood in this early period. The earliest writers on music did not consider plainchant to be 'music' as such, since it was so strongly connected to the texts which were sung that it did not occur to them to discuss the melodies in isolation. Instead, the study of music was very much an academic subject, and more like a branch of mathematics than anything to do with the performance of music. Most of this theory of music was derived from Ancient Greek and Hellenistic writers, and the main 'text-book' for music throughout the Middle Ages was a treatise entitled *De Institutione Musica* by Anicius Manlius Severinus Boethius (c.480–c.524). Boethius provided a Latin version of the Greek theories of music, which included complicated explanations of how harmony depends on geometrical proportions.

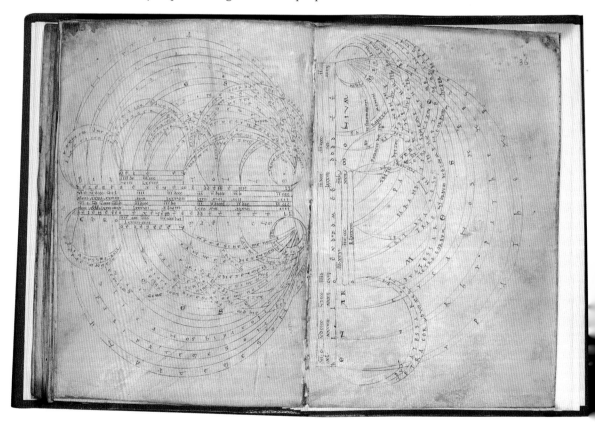

Boethius' explanation of the monochord, showing intervals as mathematical ratios. Harley MS 5237, ff. 35v-36.

In the Middle Ages, music, in this theoretical sense, was studied as one of the seven liberal arts. These were divided into a *trivium*, or group of three literary subjects: grammar, rhetoric and logic, and a *quadrivium* of four mathematical subjects:

arithmetic, geometry, astronomy and music. An illustration from the fourteenth century shows all seven of the liberal arts personified: Music, at the top, is holding open a scroll on which is written a piece in honour of Robert of Anjou, King of Naples (to whom this manuscript was presented by the people of the town of Prato in Tuscany). Next to her, Astronomy holds an instrument, while Arithmetic expounds perfect numbers and Geometry holds a triangle. Along the bottom of the page kneel the three persons of the trivium: Rhetoric lays a garland of flowers, Logic demonstrates

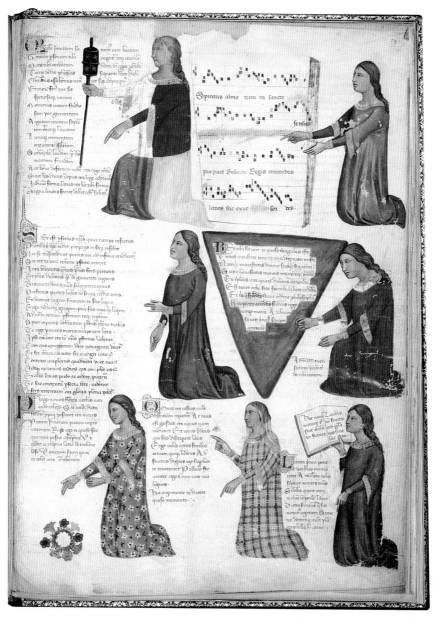

The seven Liberal Arts offer their creations to King Robert of Anjou. Royal MS 6 E IX, f. 29.

a syllogism and Grammar reads a book. Music as an academic subject thus sat happily in the company of mathematical disciplines, seemingly far away from the practicalities of musical performance.

In the Carolingian Renaissance, the revival of learning which took place in conjunction with the reforms of the Emperor Charlemagne at the start of the ninth century, there was a surge of interest in the musical theories of Boethius and other older authors. At the same time, there were attempts for the first time to link these technical theories to the practice of singing plainchant. The first to explain the workings of plainchant was Aurelian of Réôme, whose only known work, Musica Disciplina, dates from the middle of the ninth century. Aurelian's work is quite a challenge to the modern reader because he demonstrates his musical theories not with notated musical examples, but by constant reference to the words of particular chants. For a monk used to singing these chants every day, mention of the words of a chant would immediately bring to mind the melody to which it was sung, but clearly there is a limit to the amount of detailed description which can be made in this way.

It was therefore the intellectual climate of the Carolingian Renaissance which brought about the need for musical notation, partly as a way of allowing rational explanation of how music works, and partly as way of recording the new forms of

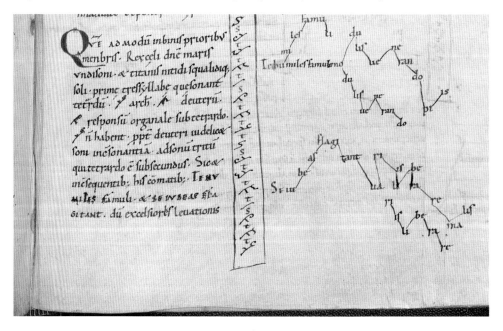

Polyphonic music in the Musica Enchiriadis treatise. Arundel MS 77, f. 70.

music which were being developed at the time. Several experimental attempts were made to represent the sound of music in writing. Some writers, again through the influence of Boethius, adopted a notation based on the letters of the alphabet, which the Ancient Greeks had used. Others used a very direct and graphic way of showing the relative pitch of notes, by writing the different syllables of the text at different heights on the page. This example (*opposite page*), taken from an eleventh-century copy of an anonymous theoretical work called *Musica Enchiriadis*, a 'music handbook' originally written in the early tenth century, shows the system in use as a way of writing down *organum*, a type of music for two separate voices. To the left of the syllables are some curious symbols showing the pitch of each line in the diagram, known as 'daseian notation' from the fact that they are based on the *daseia* sign used in Greek versification.

Though this method conveys the shape of the melody in a very direct form, it has the disadvantage of taking up a considerable amount of space, and would therefore have been prohibitively expensive for use throughout a whole book of chant. As we shall see in the next chapter, the most successful method of notation, and the one which ultimately led to the system in use by musicians today, was notation using neumes.

Music, the Liberal Art, personified. Royal MS 6 E IX, f. 29.

WRITING MUSIC

Neumes are graphic signs which indicate melodic movement. Different signs are used to show movement up or down by one note or two, or small melodic patterns such as a three-note figure moving downwards then upwards. Some signs also show expressive details, such as melodic ornaments and decorations or liquescence (when consonants such as l, m and n are treated as half-vowels). There are two basic differences between neumes and the modern system of notation: neumes do not generally indicate the rhythm of the music, and they show the pitch of notes only in relation to one another, not according to an absolute system of pitch, and without distinguishing between tones and semitones.

The very earliest neumes, which date from the second quarter of the ninth century, do not generally show the full extent of a melody. Since there had been a long tradition of singing chants without any notation, it is not particularly surprising that these early examples of notation served more as an *aide-mémoire*, to remind singers of particular details of a melody which was already familiar to them. The chief way in which chants were learned and passed down from one generation to another was by oral transmission, and this remained the case long after notation came to be commonly used. Early notation was thus a means of supporting this oral tradition, rather than a replacement to it. Indeed, for most types of notation before the twelfth century, it is impossible for us to reconstruct the precise form of the melody from the neumes alone, and we must rely on a comparison with later sources, where the notation provides fuller details.

From the very start, there was considerable variety in the forms of neumes used in different regions of Europe. To some extent this also reflected a diversity of musical and liturgical practice in plainsong across Europe. Though a few signs are found with much the same appearance in many different countries, the different families of neumes are generally classified into regional styles. One of the oldest and most widely used systems of neumes is St Gall notation, which originated in the Benedictine monastery of St Gall (or Sankt Gallen) near Lake Constance, in modern-day Switzerland. This monastery was a great artistic centre in the ninth and tenth centuries: not only did the monks attempt, for the first time, to preserve in writing

Hybrid musicians from the margin of Add. MS 47680, f.18.

what they considered to be the most authentic and pure example of chant as it had been sung in Rome; they also displayed a spirit of artistic creation which resulted in two completely new types of music for the liturgy, sequences and tropes.

The sequence, or *prosa*, is an extended composition written mainly in rhyming couplets and generally set to music with one note or neume to each syllable. It rose in the tenth century to become the musical highpoint of the mass, though it was not officially incorporated into the liturgy until some considerable time later. One of the earliest music books in the British Library is the Mainz Troper (*overleaf*), a collection of sequences and tropes written at the monastery of St Alban in Mainz in 968–972, using St Gall neumes. The main part of the pages shown here is taken up with a sequence in honour of St Gall himself, which was originally written in the 880s by the most famous author of sequence texts, Notker of St Gall. The melody of the sequence is written twice: once above the text, and again in the margin at the end of each line. Beneath this, a later scribe has written down some tropes for the mass chant 'Kyrie eleison' ('Lord, have mercy'). A trope is an introduction or interpolation to a Gregorian chant: here, for example, the words 'Lord, have mercy' are extended to 'Ineffable and unending, immense and all-powerful Lord, *have mercy*'.

The neumes in the Mainz Troper are written in a straight horizontal line, and so we cannot tell the shape of the melody from their relative position on the page. Instead, the different shapes of neumes indicate the shape of the melody. The most common signs are the *punctum*, or point (·), which is often lengthened into a *tractulus*, or short line (-), and the *virga*, from the Latin word for a rod or staff (/). The *virga* signifies that the note is higher *either* than the one preceding it *or* than the one which follows, and the *punctum* or *tractulus* can show either a lower note or a repetition of the same pitch. The choice of meaning depends on the context in which the sign occurs.

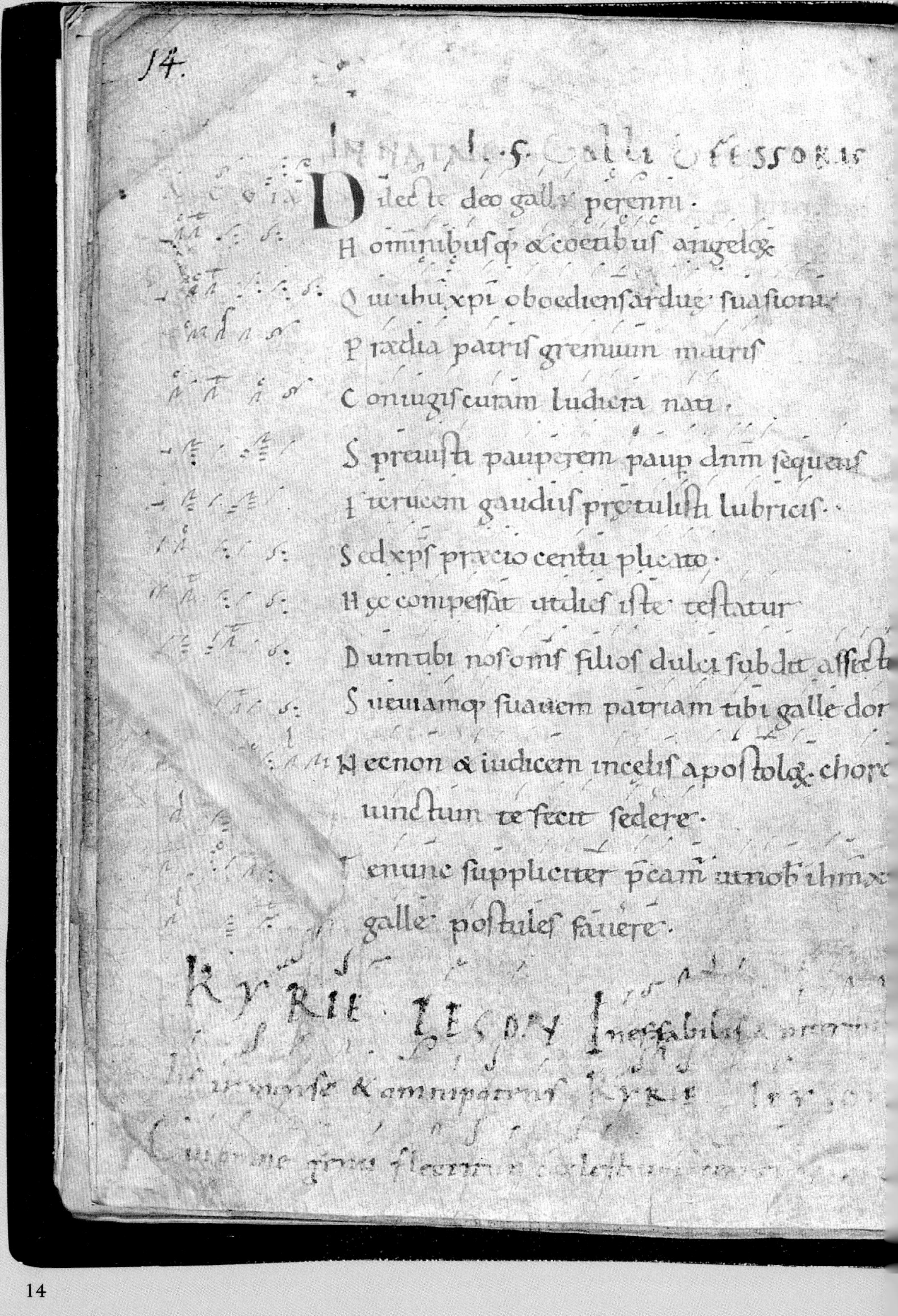

IN NATALE S. GALLI CONFESSORIS

Dilecte deo galle perenni.

Hominibusque & coetibus angelox

Quirthu xpi oboediens ardue suasionis

Pradia patris gremium matris

Coniugis curam ludicra nati

Spreuisti pauperem paup dnm sequens

terucem gaudiis pretulisti lubricas.

Sed xps pretio centu plicato.

Hec compessat utilis iste testatur

Dum tibi nos omns filios dulci subdit affect

Sueniamq suauem patriam tibi galle don

Necnon a iudicem incelis apostolox chor

iunctum te fecit sedere.

tenunc suppliciter pcam ut nob ihm x

galle postules fauere.

KYRIE LEYSON Ineffabilis

ut mense & omnipotens kyrie

Cumpne genus flecorm e celestem

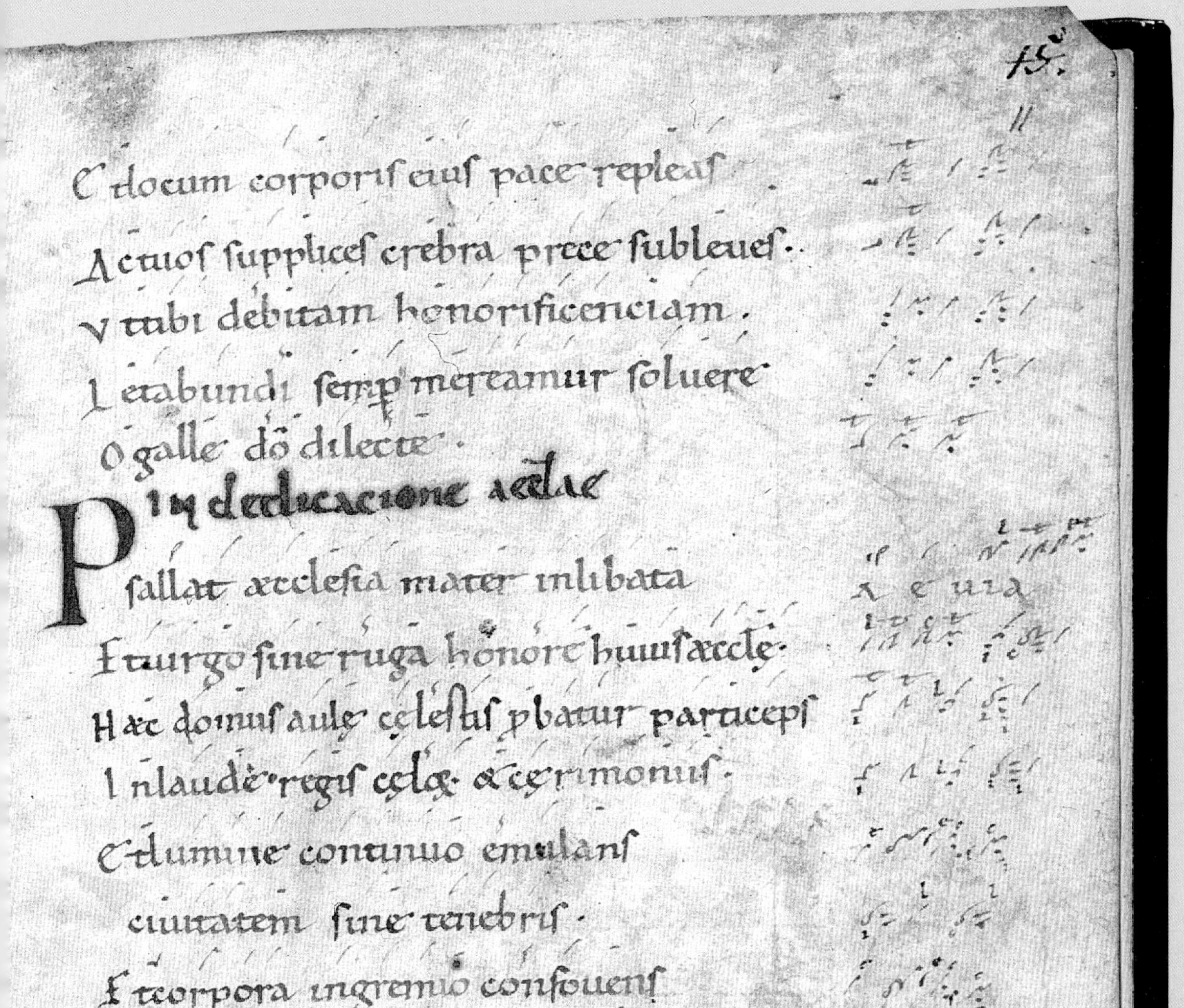

Et locum corporis eius pace repleas

Actuos supplices crebra prece subleues.

Vtibi debitam honorificenciam.

Letabundi semp mereamur soluere

O galle dõ dilecte.

P in dedicacione aeccle

Psallat aecclesia mater inlibata

Et urgo sine ruga honore huius aeccle.

Haec domus aule celestis pbatur particeps

Inlaudem regis cele acerrimonius.

Et lumine continuo emulans

ciuitatem sine tenebris.

Et corpora ingremio consouens

animarū que incelo uiuūt.

Quam dextra ptegat dei.

A laudem ipsius diu.

& insimonium KYRIE leyson

.......noster & nos opus quum factura.......

.... + XPE leyson

Sequences and Kyrie tropes in the Mainz Troper. Add. MS 19768, ff. 10v-11.

15

This is another important difference between neumatic notations and modern music notation, where the significance of each note can be understood in isolation: neumes are very dependent on other neumes around them in order to be properly understood. As well as the neumes themselves, the melodies in the margins include a few letters of the alphabet. These are known as 'significative letters' and act as abbreviations for performance directions: this illustration includes the letters t (for 'trahere' – 'drag out') and l (for 'levare' – a rise in pitch).

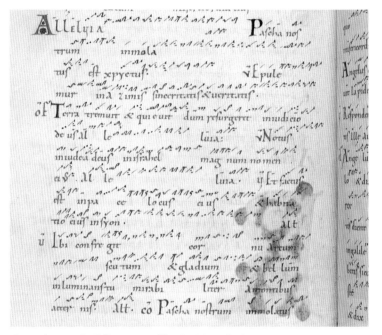

Easter chants in St Gall notation Add. MS 32247, f. 30v.

A later example of St Gall notation from Bavaria shows a much more developed state of the neumes, from the end of the eleventh century. This book is a Gradual, the liturgical book which contains all the basic chants for use in the communion service or mass – the chants which books such as the Mainz Troper were designed to supplement. On this page are the chants for the mass of Easter Day, including the chant 'Alleluia. Pascha nostrum immolatus est Christus' ('Christ our passover is sacrificed for us'; 'Christus' is written in a semi-Greek form as 'xpyctus'). Unlike in the Mainz Troper, where the sequence style generally had only one note for each syllable, in this chant there are long melismas, or streams of neumes setting one syllable of the text, such as the '–a–' of 'immolatus'. This makes the chant very elaborate, and helps to add solemnity to the feast.

The St Gall notation was used in a large area of central and eastern Europe, and had a substantial influence on later developments. By the twelfth century, when Gothic script became the predominant text hand for liturgical manuscripts, St Gall neumes were adapted to complement Gothic script. Gothic neumes are written with a wider pen and are generally more perpendicular and angular than St Gall. This example, from a twelfth-century Gradual from the Benedictine Abbey

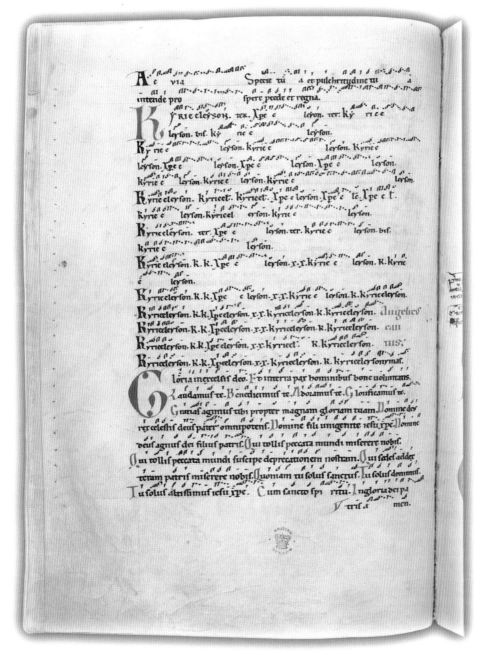

Kyriale in Gothic notation. *Add. MS 24680*, f. 49v.

of St Martin at Weingarten in Swabia, shows part of the section of the Gradual known as the 'Kyriale', which consists of the chants for the Ordinary of the Mass. The Ordinary texts are those which remain unchanged from one feast to another, the *Kyrie, Gloria, Credo, Sanctus* and *Agnus Dei*. Though none of these texts could be omitted or altered, they were varied by means of textual additions in the form of tropes, and by the use of different melodies for the standard texts. This page shows ten different melodies for the 'Kyrie eleison', each appropriate to a different class of feast or day of the week.

In the West of Europe, meanwhile, several different families of neumes are found. French sources may be categorised into four main groups. In Brittany, as well as some other parts of northern France, Breton notation was used. Breton neumes are usually written with a thicker pen than St Gall notation, and convey somewhat more precise information about pitch than St Gall neumes. On a few rare occasions this notation is also found in English sources: one example is this page from the Office of St Cuthbert, appended to a copy of the Life of St Cuthbert by the Venerable Bede. In the East of France and Belgium, Lorraine neumes were used, and in the mid-North and around Lyon a system referred to as French notation is found. In both of these systems it is common for scribes to make some attempt to indicate the relative pitch

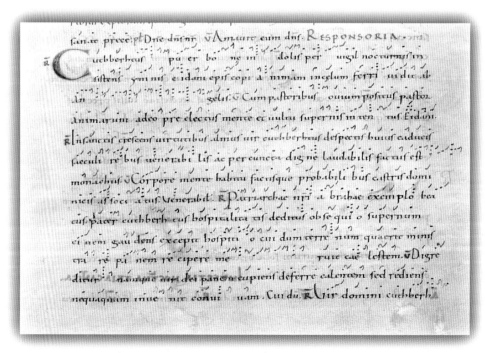

Breton Notation in an insular manuscript. Harley MS 1117, f. 43.

of notes by placing them higher or lower than one another, unlike the horizontal line used for St Gall notation.

This principle was taken further in the South of France with Aquitanian notation, which is written mainly in small points at precisely determined heights above the text. By the end of the eleventh century, when this Gradual from Toulouse was written, it had become customary to rule a line on the parchment with a dry

The Fourth Mode, from a tonary in Aquitanian notation. Harley MS 4951, f. 299v.

stylus at a mid-point between the highest and lowest notes. This served as a guide to the scribe to ensure the correct alignment of the neumes, but was also a useful means for the singer to determine the relation of different notes to one another. Though we cannot yet tell the precise form of the melody from this graph-like notation, it conveys more detailed information than the other systems. The page shown here is part of an appendix to this Gradual called the tonary. A tonary is a collection of chant melodies grouped together according to the eight modes as a reference guide to the melodies used for singing several of the more common chants. The modes are often thought of as the predecessors of the later major and minor scales, but in fact the characteristics of individual modes extend far beyond the simple choice of notes. Each mode has particular melodic formulae associated with it, and writers on music often ascribed particular moods and effects to different modes: for example, the fourth mode, as here, is often associated with bells.

Elsewhere in Europe, further distinctive forms of notation are found. The wide range of influences on Italy – from France and Germany on northern Italy, from Normandy on Sicily and from Greece on the South – each played a part in forming a diverse range of musical forms, the most distinctive of which was the Beneventan notation (*below*). The Iberian Peninsula had remained fiercely independent of Rome until 1085, when the Mozarabic Rite was finally suppressed and Gregorian chant came to be used. The notation used for this old Spanish rite in the provinces of Castile and León is very characteristic, with long, almost vertical strokes instead of the oblique lines found in most other regions, and very ornate curves (*opposite page, left*). This page shows a chant for St John the Baptist in a tenth- or eleventh-century book from the Abbey of Silos which contains chants for both the mass and the office. A later hand has added several 'Alleluia' melodies in the empty space of the margin.

In England, we have already seen that Breton notation was occasionally used. Far more common, though, is a notation which bears much similarity with the northern French notation, especially with sources associated with the Abbey of Corbie, which exerted a considerable influence on English manuscript

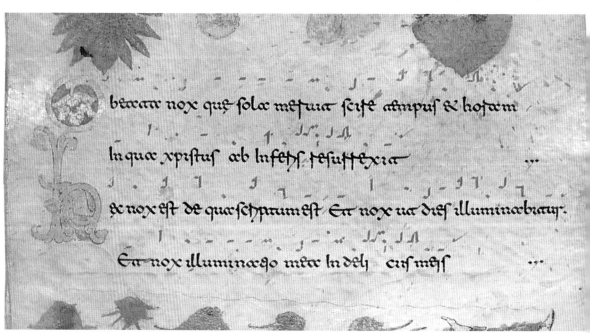

Beneventan notation from the Exultet roll illustrated on page 49. Add. MS 30337.

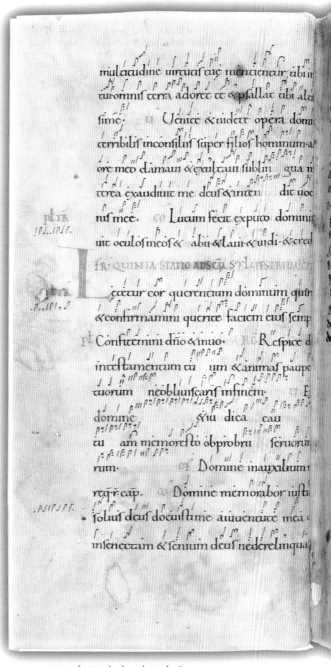

Visigothic neumes in a chant for St John the Baptist.
Add. MS 30845, f. 13.

Part of a Gradual with Anglo-Saxon neumes.
Harley MS 110, f. 1v.

production before the Norman Conquest. This style of writing, known as Anglo-Saxon notation, is characterised by its neat, long and perpendicular neume-forms which make full use of the space between text-lines, despite being written essentially in a straight line, not at different heights to reflect the shape of the melody (*above right*).

Overleaf: the Naming of John the Baptist from the Cotton Troper. Cotton MS Caligula A XIV, ff. 20v-21.

DUM POSCIT LOQUITUR · DNM BENEDICENDO PRECATUR

SIC PUELLAR · PATER HUNC POSCIT VOCITARI

IN NATIVITATE S IOHIS BAP

Iohannes est hic domini pre

cursor cui laude xpi cantemus honorem di

centes De uentre. Post longeuam sterilitaté

mirabiliter foecundatam Vocauit Quod an

te mundi constitutionem presciuit & prede

stinauit. Et posuit. ALII.

De utero genitricis mee me uocauit deus meus

meo nomine. De uentre. Ad uiuorum capita

triumphaliter abscidenda. Vocauit. Ne hosti

lis inmanitas superare me. Et posuit. Valen

uorem facie meam omniu uultibus potenti

um reddens. Sub tegumto. Bonu est. ITE

Que prophete predixere agni fore precurso

rem. De uentre. Honestauit uerbu suum ore

meo. Et posuit. Construens me sup gentes

atque regna. Posuit me. Gloria. ALII

Valtu firma fides regis baptista iohannes. ex

utero sterili narrant preconia xpi. De uentre.

Post longu senium inspirato germine foete.

Vocauit. Qui quondam moysi dixit te exno

One of the most important manuscripts to use Anglo-Saxon notation is the Cotton Troper, a richly illuminated collection possibly made in Winchester in the second half of the eleventh century (*previous pages*). This opening shows the tropes for the feast of St John the Baptist, with a depiction of the naming of John. Unlike the 'Kyrie eleison' tropes in the Mainz Troper (*pages 14–15*), this trope consists of interpolations to a chant specific to the feast of St John the Baptist, the chant for the introit of the mass, 'De ventre matris meae vocavit me Dominus' ('The Lord has called me from my mother's womb'). The trope elements were probably sung by a solo singer in between each phrase of the main chant, which was sung by the choir. Because the Troper is a soloist's book, the main chant is not written out in full, since the choir would have sung from their own book, the Gradual. Instead, only the first word or two of each phrase of the main chant is written ('De ventre', 'Vocavit', etc.), to indicate the correct placing of the tropes.

In the course of time, it came to be considered that the amount of information conveyed by each of these systems of neumes was insufficient. A neume might show that a note should be higher than the preceding one, but would not specify whether this meant a tone or a semitone higher. First attempts at making the shape of the melody clearer involved placing the neumes at different heights on the page, as with Aquitanian notation, but using a variety of different neume-forms instead of predominantly single dots. An example is this twelfth-century Troper from Normandy (*opposite*). Further precision came with the addition of ruled lines to show the

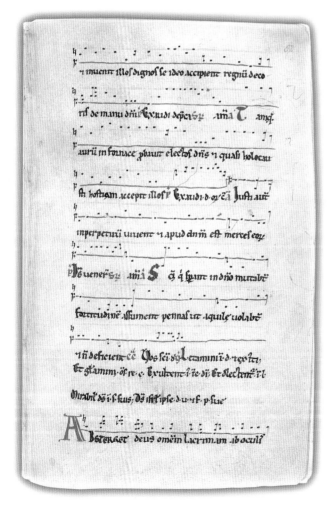

Ruled F and C lines in the Lyon Diurnal. Add. MS 17302, f. 52.

height of notes of particular pitches. In this monastic Diurnal (*page 24*), a book containing the texts of the daytime services used by Carthusian monks in the province of Lyon, a red line shows the pitch F, and a yellow line shows the placement of C

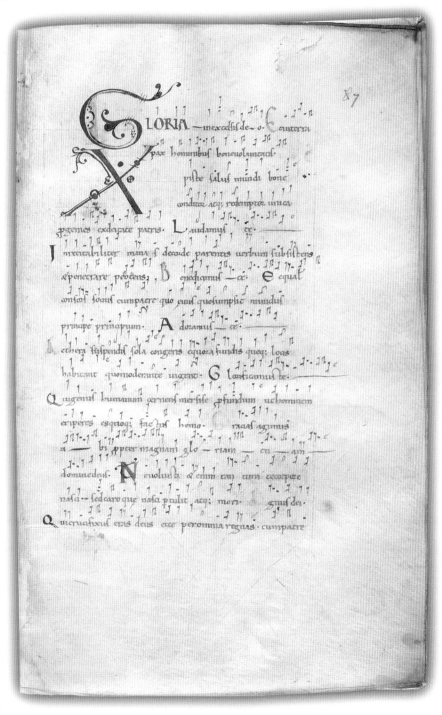

A troped Gloria with heightened neumes. Royal MS 8 C XIII, f. 7.

above it. The letter 'F' and a 'B natural' sign are written as guides at the start of each stave, from which it is possible to name each note on the page, and to make an accurate transcription into modern notation.

The final stage in this progression towards unequivocal accuracy was to have not two lines, but four. In this Gradual and Troper from St Alban's Abbey from later in the twelfth century there is no guiding letter 'F', but again a natural sign between the second and third lines shows that this space is a B natural. (In the bottom line this changes to a B flat at the word 'cuncta'.) The four-line stave came to be used in almost

A troped Gloria on
a four-line stave.
Royal MS 2 B IV, f. 24v.

all music books from the thirteenth century onwards. A stave of five or even six lines was used in some cases where the range of notes extended too far to fit onto four lines, as happens in the famous 'Sumer is icumen in', which is discussed later. This was more common in instrumental than vocal music at first, but by the sixteenth century the five-line stave was used for almost all music except plainchant, which usually retained its traditional style of four lines. During the time when the stave came into common use, from the end of the twelfth into the thirteenth century, neume forms throughout Europe generally began to become squarer in form, in keeping

The rota 'Sumer is icumen in'.
Harley MS 978, f. 11v.

Qui cherubin mystice imitamur & uiuifice trinitati ter sanctum
ymnum offerimus Omnem nunc mundanam deponamus sollici
tudinem Sicuti regem omnium suscepturi Cui ab angelicis inuisi
biliter ministratur cuius ordo   alleluia ΑΛΛΗΛΙΑ

Te igitur precordiorum uocis Te precamur trinitas sanctum
domine sabaoth qui reples mundum gloria tua ut corda biora
nostra reples laude tua. Quicumque cum angelis ad uis te
cum sanctis pueris tuis acuncis purificati uius digne clica
mus Osanna in excelsis   Hac est fides catho
lica ut unum deum in trinitate   ... ... con
munione ueneremur. ... ...

Domine iesu xpe rex glorie libera animas omnium defunctorum
de manu inferni & de profundo laci libera eas & feat leonis ne ab
sorbeat eas tartarus ne cadunt in obscurum: Sed signifer lanc
cus michahel representet eas in lucem sanctam quam olim
Abrahe promisisti & se-   ... ...
ΑΕ

Nec xpe resurgens & mortuis iam non moritur mors illi ti mondam
nabitur

with the Gothic system of scripts which became prevalent at the same time, and by the end of the thirteenth century the familiar 'square-note' form of notation had become virtually uniform across western Europe.

The Greek Orthodox Church, and indeed the whole of Byzantine civilisation, was of course largely detached from the practices of the western church throughout the Middle Ages, but there are several interesting examples of influence between the two churches. Much of the theory of western music, not least the idea and the terminologies of the modal system, was derived from Greek writings. There are also a few rare occurrences of Byzantine chants being translated into Latin. One of the most important Greek chants is the 'Cheroubikon', which is sung at the ceremony of the Great Entrance in the Orthodox liturgy. This chant is found unexpectedly in a Latin translation on a blank page in a tenth-century collection of writings of Boethius from the Rhineland (left). The reason for its appearance in this manuscript is very unclear, but it is at least possible that it was included for use in some context within the western mass.

The Byzantine liturgy had its own quite independent system of notation, a reformed version of which remains in use in the Greek Church to this day. Byzantine notation was somewhat later in reaching a fully developed and decipherable state than its western counterparts: the earliest use of signs to show melodic movement is in the tenth century, but by the thirteenth century a fully developed system had emerged which continued to be used until the nineteenth century. This notation shows considerably more interpretational nuance than any of the western systems in use in the Middle Ages. For example, there are no fewer than six different signs for a single ascending note, each implying a different sort of stress or ornamentation.

The choir books of the eastern church correspond, at least at a general level, with those of the West. There are several different books for the music of the divine liturgy (the equivalent of the western mass) and the morning and evening offices of lauds and vespers, each designed for different participants in the services. This page (overleaf) is from a thirteenth-century Sticherarion, a book of stichera, or hymns for these morning and evening offices. It is from the start of the second section of the book, called the 'Triodion', which contains the stichera for the ten weeks leading up to Easter, beginning with the Sunday of the Pharisee and the Publican.

The Russian Orthodox Church used neumes based on an earlier and less precise version of the Byzantine system, and developed them very little through the

29

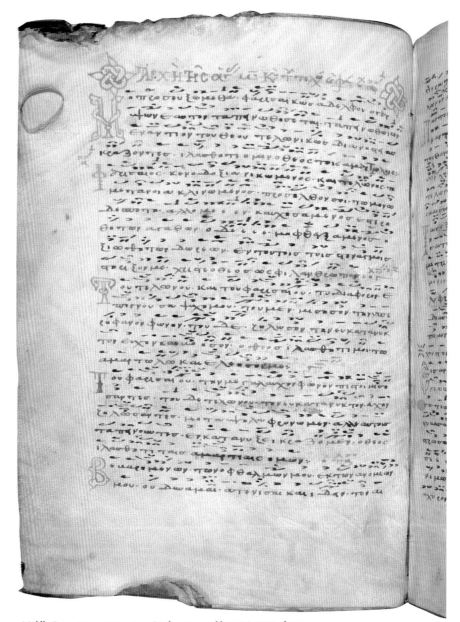

Middle Byzantine notation in a Sticherarion. Add. MS 27865, f. 56v.

medieval period. For this reason, though it is possible to transcribe and perform Byzantine chant from the thirteenth century onwards, our knowledge of the precise melodies of Slavonic chant from the same period is much less clear. Other eastern churches used quite independent systems: one example is the Armenian *khaz* notation, which again shows not only melodic movement but also rhythmic and expressive details (*opposite*). This page, with a typically ornamental headpiece, shows a hymn for the feast of the Lighting of the Lamps.

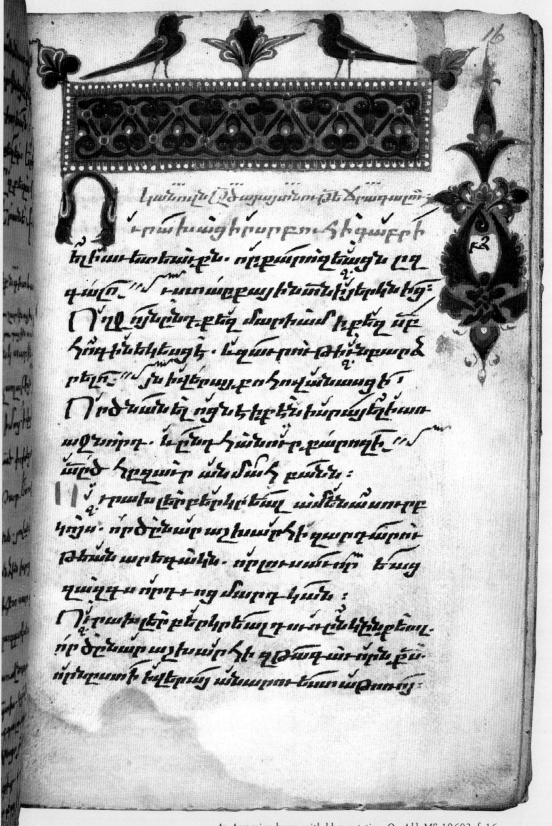

An Armenian hymn with khaz notation. Or. Add. MS 18603, f. 16.

NEW FORMS OF MUSIC

The preceding chapter was concerned more with the notation of music than with music itself. Most of the examples were taken from manuscripts of the tenth to twelfth centuries, the time during which notation developed from being a few signs to remind singers of specific details of a melody which was already known to them, into a sophisticated and accurate system of denoting small details of interpretation. Through these centuries, some aspects of the music itself remained remarkably constant. Indeed, the very act of writing down the melodies of plainchant served as a way of codifying and standardising chants which had previously been subject to local variation. Through the same period, however, there had also been a strong tradition of experimenting with new forms of music. As we have seen, tropes and sequences, neither of which formed part of the official canonical books of the liturgy, came to assume an ever more important role in embellishing and adding grandeur to the mass.

The unprecedented accuracy of square notation on a four-line stave was a considerable help in accelerating the development of new musical styles. Because the stave allows one to see exactly where two notes stand in relation to one another, it is perfectly suited to recording polyphonic music, in which two or more different melodies are sung simultaneously. Normally one part, called the *tenor*, or leading voice, sings the plainsong melody, with other voices elaborating above it. Such music had certainly been in existence in previous centuries, but there had been only few attempts to write it down using the older forms of notation. Some of the evidence for early polyphony lies in the musical examples given in theory books from the ninth century onwards (*page 10*), which hint that the additional voices were improvised from an early stage but not usually written down. One important manuscript of polyphony from Winchester survives from the eleventh century, but it was the advent of the stave at the end of the twelfth century which did most to promote its development into a written art-form. One centre for polyphony in the twelfth century was the monastery of St Martial de Limoges, and this source (*opposite*) seems to have been written somewhere nearby in Aquitaine or Catalunya. The two vocal parts are clearly separated by a red line drawn between them, and each melodic line is written

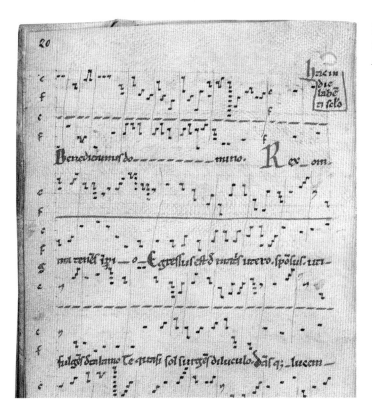

Two-part polyphony of the twelfth century. Add. MS 36881, f. 10v.

in square notes on a stave ruled with a dry point, with the letters c and f at the start of each line to show the pitches. This piece is a polyphonic trope of the words 'Benedicamus Domino'.

By the first half of the thirteenth century, ways of writing down polyphonic music had developed rapidly, and the conductus shown (overleaf) can be transcribed into modern notation with much greater accuracy than the earlier examples. Conductus is a term used to describe a range of different types of medieval Latin song. This example is for three voices, and the three staves are clearly separated on the page by being ruled in different colours. The manuscript from which it comes was made at the Cathedral of Beauvais, and includes two exceptionally important musical items. This piece is taken from one of the more extraordinary events in the liturgy as it was celebrated in Beauvais. In the days after Christmas in this and several other cathedrals and large churches, the hierarchy of the church was temporarily overturned. On St Stephen's Day (26 December) the deacons led the services, on St John's Day (27 December) the priests, and Holy Innocents' Day (28 December) was organised by the choir-boys, with one of their number elected Boy Bishop. The feast most often

A three-part arrangement of the Song of the Ass. Egerton MS 2615, ff. 43v-44.

dammas et capreolos super dromedarios velox

medyanos hez. Dum trahit vehicula multa

cum sarcinula illius mandibula dura terit

pabula. hez. Dum aristis ordeum comedit

. 42 .

35

The beginning of the
Danielis Ludus of Beauvais.
Egerton MS 2615, f. 95.

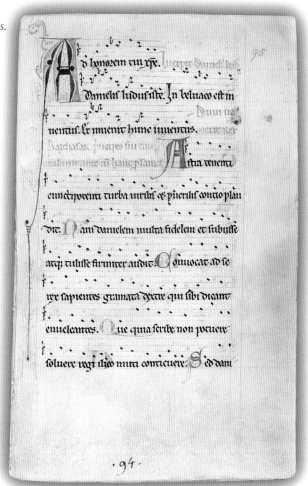

The beginning of the
Danielis Ludus of Beauvais.
Egerton MS 2615, f. 95.

condemned by the church authorities, however, was the feast of the sub-deacons and other lower ranks, which usually took place on the day of the Circumcision (1 January). At Beauvais these celebrations included leading a girl on an ass into the Cathedral, representing the flight into Egypt, and the congregation would bray like an ass at all the important moments in the liturgy. This song of the ass, which begins with the words 'Orientis partibus', was sung before the reading of the Epistle at the mass, and each verse ends with the refrain 'Hez, sir asne, hez!'

The other important item in this manuscript is the *Danielis Ludus*, or *Play of Daniel*, one of the most substantial of several types of liturgical drama which survive from the Middle Ages. The individual characters' parts, which tell the story of Daniel as a prophecy of the coming of Christ, are set to music throughout, and detailed instructions for the performance of the play, some hinting at instruments, are given in rubrics, the directions written in red ink. This page (*opposite*) shows the beginning of the play. The rubric states that 'as King Belshazzar comes forth, his princes sing this song before him', at which the chorus comes forward singing the story of the play.

The Beauvais manuscript dates from around 1230, and is very accurately notated in terms of pitch and, in the case of the polyphonic song of the ass, the relation between the three voices, but the notation is still quite imprecise as far as rhythm is concerned (though a certain amount can be conjectured from the rhythm of the poetry). Through the thirteenth century, however, rhythm became an increasingly important aspect of new composition, especially in polyphonic genres such as the motet. In contrast to plainchant, or *musica plana*, which continued to be sung without a regular beat, the new *musica mensurabilis*, or measured music, depended increasingly on repeated rhythmic patterns, which led ultimately to the use of regular bars or measures. This example (*below*) shows a three-part setting of 'Kyrie eleison' from the early fourteenth century, by which time quite a range of different rhythms can be seen in the variety of different note-shapes used. Another century later, considerably more sophistication was possible, as can be seen in this setting of the chorus parts of St Luke's Passion from the Windsor Carol Book (*overleaf*). Several notes

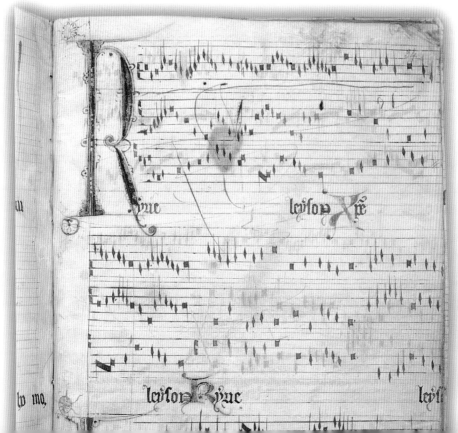

Rhythmic notation of the ars nova. Arundel MS 14, f. 34.

37

A three-part setting of the title and crowd parts of the St Luke Passion. Egerton MS 3307, f. 20.

have ascending tails – the ancestor of the modern crotchet or quarter note – and there are also some notes written in red, which again has significance for the rhythm. This manuscript, as well as including the earliest polyphonic settings of the Passion, is one of the main sources of Christmas carols of the fifteenth century. It was probably written for St George's Chapel, Windsor, between 1430 and 1444, though some have suggested a connection with Meaux Abbey in Yorkshire.

All of the new developments so far discussed took place within the context of the Christian liturgy. The thirteenth and fourteenth centuries were also, however, a time when music from other traditions first came to be written down. Folk music, and indeed most forms of instrumental music, continued to be passed down without the use of writing (as we shall see in the final chapter), but other forms of secular music-making began to put the notation developed within the church to their own purposes. There had been a long tradition of more learned secular verse sung to music, both in Latin and in vernacular languages, but it was rare for the music to be written into the manuscripts. Furthermore, in cases where music was written down, such as the famous *Carmina Burana* manuscript written in the 1220s, it was quite common for the notation to be much less detailed and informative than it was in contemporary liturgical manuscripts. In late twelfth and thirteenth-century France, the Troubadours (in the South) and Trouvères (in the North) were sophisticated poet-musicians who refined and developed the idea of courtly love, using great subtlety in their artistic expression. For almost the first time in music history, it became common for the composers' names to be written in the manuscripts. This Trouvère manuscript (*overleaf*) includes some nineteen songs in French, and this song about a nightingale's voice is attributed in the margin to Reignaut, the Chastelain de Couci.

Comparable artistry is found in the German *Minnesang* and in the *Cantigas de Santa María* written by King Alfonso 'el Sabio' in the Galician language. There was no such tradition in the British Isles at this time, but evidence does survive of other types of music-making outside the liturgy. The most famous example of vernacular medieval song in English is the *rota*, or round, 'Sumer is icumen in' (*page 27*). This composition is an isolated work in a compilation volume of the mid-thirteenth century, probably from Reading Abbey, containing amongst other things Goliardic poetry and medical texts. Four singers sing the same melody one after the other, each starting when the previous singer reaches the red cross on the first line, while two

A trouvère song in Old French. Egerton MS 274, ff. 108v-109.

lower voices repeat the words 'Sing cuccu' to the notes written underneath. Copious instructions of how to perform the round are given in the bottom right section of the page, and an alternative sacred text in Latin, 'Perspice Christicola', is provided for use in other contexts.

As musical notation came increasingly to be used for secular vocal music in vernacular languages, so too was it used for instrumental music. The same Reading manuscript is very interesting in containing three instrumental compositions. The instruments to be used are not specified, and the music is stylistically close to forms of vocal polyphony from the time. There is also a small amount of keyboard music in a book from Robertsbridge Abbey in Sussex dating from the second quarter of the fourteenth century (*opposite*). While music for string and wind instruments generally used similar notation to vocal music, the earliest keyboard notation was written in a form of shorthand called tablature. This piece is very probably intended for the organ. The top line of the music is written on a stave with customary note-forms, while the notes of the chords underneath are written as letters. Rests are shown by the letter 's' (for *sine*, 'without'), and the duration of notes is determined by comparison with the upper part. Both of these examples are exceptionally early, and it was not until much later in the fourteenth century that it became reasonably common for instrumental music to be written down.

The most important of all late medieval music manuscripts in England is the Old Hall Manuscript, named after St Edmund's College, Old Hall Green, near Ware in Hertfordshire, where the manuscript was kept between 1893 and 1973. The bulk of the volume was compiled around 1415–20, with several later additions in the 1420s, and its particular importance lies in the fact that for most pieces the names of composers are given. Named composers are known in particular contexts from throughout the preceding century, but this

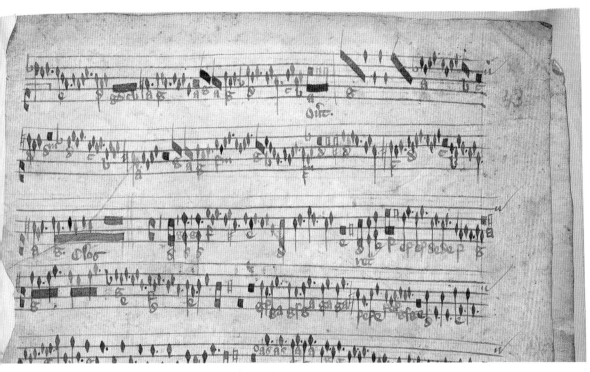

The earliest notated keyboard music. Add. MS 28550, f. 43.

manuscript can be seen as the first in the tradition of naming composers for the sake of identifying unique stylistic characteristics of individual artists. This page (*opposite*) shows one part of a setting of the Gloria (the other two vocal parts are written on the following page) attributed to 'Roy Henry', who is most likely to be King Henry V. As in the Windsor Carol Book, some notes are coloured red to show a proportional relation with the duration of black notes. Other pieces also use blue and void notes, and a wide range of interdependent time signatures, to create highly sophisticated rhythmic effects of a complexity not subsequently encountered in music until the twentieth century.

Opposite: part of the Gloria by Roy Henry from the Old Hall Manuscript. Add. MS 57950, f. 12v.

Et in terra pax hominibus bo ne volunta tis. Lau

damus te benedicimus te Adoramus te glorificamus te gracias

agimus tibi propter magnam gloriam tuam. Domine de us rex ce

lestis deus pa ter omnipotens domine fi li unigenite ihu ari ste. Dom

ne deus agnus de i filius pa tris. Qui tollis peccata mundi

miserere re no bis. Qui tollis peccata mundi suscipe deprecationem

no stram. Qui sedes ad dexteram pa tris miserere no bis.

Quoniam tu so lus sanctus. Tu solus do minus. Tu so lus al tissimus

Ihesu xriste cum sancto spiritu in gloria de i pa tris. A

Antiphonal psalmody in an Office for the Dead. Egerton MS 1070, f. 54v.

SINGING AND PLAYING MUSIC

In the preceding survey of the development of notation from the tenth to the fifteenth centuries, the illustrations have been taken from a remarkably wide range of different types of book. We can tell a great deal about the contexts in which the music was performed from the type of book in which it occurs. The various participants in the mass – the celebrant, deacon and sub-deacon, the cantor or choir and the congregation or monastic community – each had different chants to sing, and this is reflected in the different sorts of music found in the various books used in the liturgy. It was common for several chants, especially psalms, to be sung antiphonally, with two choirs singing alternate verses from either side of the church. This practice is shown in a picture of the office of the dead from an early fifteenth-century Book of Hours of King René of Anjou (*opposite*), where two groups of singers are shown singing from books. We can tell a certain amount about the numbers of singers involved in different types of music-making both from pictures such as this and from the physical size of different books. Only one singer could have sung from a small book such as the Mainz Troper (*pages* 14–15; the pages measure 17 x 13 cm), whereas Antiphoners were usually large enough for several singers to share between them. By the fifteenth century, some chant books had reached unprecedentedly large proportions. This Sienese hymnal measures 42 x 29 cm (others are considerably larger still), and the notation within it

A Sienese choirbook with bosses and straps.
Add. MS 30014.

is so large that the book could be opened on a lectern and seen by a large number of singers standing some distance away (page 52 shows an illumination from this book).

In other cases, the context in which the music is found makes it unlikely that it was performed directly from the book. Some of the earliest sources of polyphonic music seem to be intended to preserve the way the music was performed as a record on parchment for the sake of posterity, and might therefore be termed 'library copies'. At other times, music is written into what certainly are library books. These Alleluia melodies have been added to a blank half-page at the end of a chapter of Bede's Life of St Cuthbert (below). They do not have any obvious relevance to the rest of the book, and yet seem too neatly written to be simply a copying exercise by a scribe learning the forms of neumes.

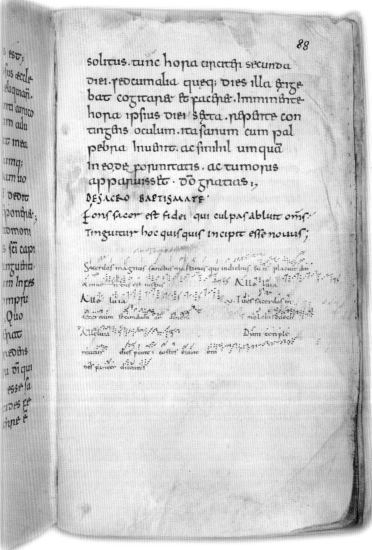

Chants added to a spare half-page of parchment.
Cotton MS Vitellius A XIX, f.88.

Three clerics sing the motet 'Zelo tui langueo' from a roll.
Arundel MS 83, f. 63v.

Singers interpreting with hand-movements.
Harley MS 2888, f. 98v.

A more easily portable and less costly format for disseminating music was the roll. This illustration from the East Anglian Howard Psalter (*above left*) shows three clerics singing a well-known motet, 'Zelo tui langueo', from a roll, while one of them carries another roll wound up. Illustrations of this type are often found (as here) in Psalters, within the illuminated initial letter 'C' of Psalm 97 (98 in the English numbering), 'Cantate Domino canticum novum' ('Sing unto the Lord a new song'), and can offer interesting insights into the ways in which music was performed. In the Howard Psalter, two of the singers hold a hand to one ear so that they can better hear how their own voices blend with the others, a practice employed by unaccompanied vocal groups to this day. In another case (*above right*) one singer directs the music by means of hand movements.

Only a few rolls such as those depicted above survive today, since it is by its nature a less permanent format than the codex, and was therefore used more for ephemeral compositions than for the standard chants of the liturgy. There was one exceptional case of a roll being used within the liturgy, in the vigil mass of Easter as it was celebrated in the South of Italy, especially in and around Benevento. Before the mass proper, after the new fire of Easter had been brought into the church, the

The Exultet roll unrolled from the pulpit. Add. MS 30337.

deacon would sing a lengthy chant from a roll, known as the Exultet roll after the first word of the chant written upon it. As he proceeded with the chant, the deacon would unwind the roll over the pulpit, and it would gradually fall from the pulpit to the ground (*above*). Many of the surviving rolls are richly illuminated with pictures referring to the narrative of the chant, and the illustrations are painted upside down in relation to the text, so that they would be seen the right way up by the congregation as the roll unwound down the front of the pulpit (*opposite*). This roll, one of the finest surviving examples, extends to some 22½ feet when fully unwound.

Not all musical pictures in liturgical manuscripts show music being used within the liturgy, however. Some of our most important iconographical information about musical instruments comes from pictures illustrating chants which would never have been accompanied by instruments. Indeed, the wealth of pictorial information about secular music-making found in the margins and illuminations of chant books goes some way to restoring the gaps in our knowledge left by the dearth of written sources of secular music. Great care is required, however, when making judgements about the construction of instruments and the contexts in which they were used, since a wide range of extra-musical matters have to be taken into consideration. Manuscript artists were often more concerned to reproduce images according to accepted styles and genres of illumination than to reproduce exact scale drawings of the instruments they knew, and the degree of elaboration in their pictures could often have more to do with the patronage under which the manuscript was produced than the relative sophistication of the instruments around at the time of production.

King David was the most famous musician of the Old Testament, and images of him are frequently found, either playing the lyre (*frontispiece and page 58*) or the organ (*title page*), or in the company of musicians, as in an image of David worshipping before the ark of the covenant (*page 4*). It could be that the illustration from the Vespasian Psalter (*frontispiece*) shows the artist's deliberately archaic idea of a lyre from Biblical times, in keeping with the simple ramshorns at his side, whereas the artist of the much later Book of Hours (*page 4*) was keen to show the latest models of trumpets and stringed

Exultet Roll with Beneventan notation and inverted pictures. Add. MS 30337.

instruments. In fact, however, it is unlikely that either artist had actual instruments before him to act as inspiration: each was instead intending to represent simple types of instrument according to the stylistic customs of his time.

The illustration of David before the ark does, though, show more than simply a collection of instruments. The two halves of the page clearly demonstrate the division between 'loud' and 'soft' categories of instruments. The majestic trumpets saluting the ark are contrasted with the quieter instruments below: a portative organ, a long flute, a lute and a small harp. Other evidence, in contemporary writings and from later practice, shows that quiet or loud instruments would be played together, but that it was not customary to mix the two categories. With this in mind, it is likely that the assortment of musicians filling the arcade at the bottom of this page of the Barcelona Haggadah (below) was painted with the intention of showing a

Musicians play while putti point their trumpets towards an ornate mazzah. Or. Add. MS 14761, f. 61.

representative selection of instrumentalists rather than an actual musical ensemble. From left to right are shown a pipe and tabor (a common combination for one player to play simultaneously), a rebec (a violin-like instrument with a vaulted back), a lute, bagpipes and small kettle-drums.

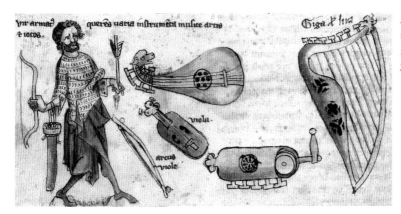

A pictorial catalogue: the unnamed instrument is a hurdy-gurdy. Sloane MS 3983, f. 13.

Our knowledge of the names of these instruments is mainly drawn from documentary sources, but on rare occasions their names are given in the picture itself (*above*). Another illustration (*below*), accompanying John Lydgate's translation of Guillaume de Deguileville's *The Pilgrimage of the Life of Man*, shows three instruments described in the poem:

> I sawgh one that blewe an horn
> And mayde a noysë wonder lowde;
> And as I espyen koude,
> In organys and in sawtrye
> She made a wonder melodye.

A well-furnished music room. Cotton MS Tiberius A VII, f. 104v.

The 'sawtrye', or psaltery, is a type of zither, with strings strung across a wooden box with soundholes, normally played horizontally, either with the fingers or with plectra.

Elsewhere, pictures of musical instruments can have a more symbolic role. The large Sienese hymnary shown above (*page 45*) includes this splendid array of a heavenly choir and orchestra surrounding the Blessed Virgin Mary and accompanying the gold notation of the hymn *Ave Maris Stella* (*below and page 61*), while a slightly earlier Italian manuscript shows a range of more worldly instruments as an illustration to a treatise on the vices (*opposite*). Again it is unlikely that either artist drew these images with the intention of showing precisely lifelike instruments, but both pictures give

The angelic orchestra praises the Virgin while (opposite) worldly musicians enrich a den of vice. Add. MS 30014, f. 124v; Add. MS 27695, f. 13.

A 'soft consort' of lute, recorder and harp. Harley MS 4375, f. 151v.

an idea of the range of different types of instrument around at the time of their creation. The heavenly orchestra has the primary aim of glorifying the Virgin, but also a subsidiary aim of adding prestige to the order of Augustinian canons for whom the book was written.

Other pictures can convey more specific information about the social context in which different types of music were performed. An earlier picture (*page 47*) showed three tonsured clerics singing a motet, and what little we know about the provenance of sources of this type of motet suggests that this is a typical setting in which to find such music. Such pieces were apparently written by and for small groups of highly-educated singers, usually in holy orders, to perform for their own amusement. The well-dressed trio in another illustration (*above*) are surrounded in a small room by books, showing an educated and refined context for this type of instrumental ensemble. Again the music-making seems to be more of a pastime for cultured amateurs than a performance by professional musicians. Some of the rustic musicians from the margins of the Luttrell Psalter give a vivid impression of music-making in the countryside (*above right*).

Musicians and dancers in the margins of the Luttrell Psalter. Add. MS 42130, f. 164v.

Their instruments are far simpler in construction than the elegantly designed instruments of the previous illustration, but here too it is likely that these musicians play for enjoyment rather than for a living. Their dancing is spontaneous and lively, quite unlike the formal atmosphere of this courtly gathering in a well-tended arboretum (*below*), which shows two singers, one with a psaltery, which he plucks with both hands, and the other playing a lute, apparently using a plectrum. In this case the music is clearly being performed by professional musicians as an entertainment for the queen

A courtly music party. Add. MS 12228, f. 222v.

and her entourage, and we might imagine such a setting for the performance of the trouvère song discussed earlier (*page 40*).

These pictures portray music-making as an enjoyable pastime, but many more illustrations show the purposeful or ceremonial functions of music, either as a vehicle of praise or foreboding, or as a means of adding dignity to a public occasion. The trumpeters illustrating the Book of Joel (*half-title page*) are sounding an alarm to foretell the coming of the Lord. (It is worth noting that their puffed out cheeks are characteristic of many medieval pictures of trumpeters, and point to a different method of playing from that normally used today.) In another Biblical scene, this time from a fifteenth-century history of the Bible written in Flemish, a public procession of instruments is shown. Such a use of music in outdoor processions is well attested in the fifteenth century and later, though the use of soft instruments as

A large group of musicians in procession. Add. MS 38122, f. 90.

well as the more appropriate loud instruments may be more accountable to artistic licence than to actual practice.

It is important to remember that each one of these pictures is above all a work of art. If we are to reap full benefit from the evidence presented by manuscript illuminations, then we must be as fully aware as possible of the contexts in which their artists created them. Pictures of instruments go a good way towards filling some of the gaps left in our knowledge by the dearth of notated instrumental music, but the information which they provide demands an extra level of caution on the part of the modern scholar.

An aspiring fiddle player.
Stowe MS 17, f. 145v.

FURTHER READING

The New Grove Dictionary of Music and Musicians
(London, 1980, 2nd ed., 2001), especially the substantial
articles on 'Notation' and 'Sources, MS'.

The New Oxford History of Music, vol. 2: *The Early Middle Ages to 1300*,
ed. Richard Crocker and David Hiley (2nd ed., Oxford, 1989)
and vol. 3: *Ars Nova and the Renaissance, 1300–1540*, ed. Gerald
Abraham and Anselm Hughes (Oxford, 1963).

David Hiley, *Western Plainchant: a Handbook* (Oxford, 1993).

Tess Knighton and David Fallows, eds., *A Companion to Medieval
and Renaissance Music* (London, 1992).

David Munrow, *Instruments of the Middle Ages and Renaissance*
(Oxford, 1976).

The quarterly journal *Early Music* (London, 1973–)
has frequent articles on medieval music and musicians,
often richly illustrated.

The German series *Musikgeschichte in Bildern* (Leipzig, 1961–)
includes several volumes devoted to pictures of medieval
music and musicians.

LISTENING

Florilège grégorien, I-II.
Chœur des Moines de Solesmes, dir. Dom Jean Claire.
Solesmes CD S829/S838.

Musique et poésie à Saint-Gall: sequences et tropes du IXe siècle.
Ensemble Gilles Binchois, dir. Dominique Vellard.
Harmonia Mundi 905239, 1997.

Les premières polyphonies françaises: organa et tropes du XIe siècle.
Ensemble Gilles Binchois, dir. Dominique Vellard.
Virgin Veritas 5 45135 2, 1996.

English Songs of the Middle Ages.
Sequentia, dir. Benjamin Bagby.
Harmonia Mundi GD 77019, 1989.

*The Marriage of Heaven and Hell: Motets and Songs from Thirteenth-Century
France.*
Gothic Voices, dir. Christopher Page.
Hyperion CDA66423, 1990.

The Old Hall Manuscript.
Hilliard Ensemble, dir. Paul Hillier.
EMI Reflexe 54111/ Virgin Edition 61393, 1990.

Ludus Danielis.
The Harp Consort, dir. Andrew Lawrence-King.
Deutsche Harmonia Mundi 77395, 1997.

Left: joyful musicians from the Book of Psalms. Harley MS 2804, f. 3v

LIST OF MANUSCRIPTS ILLUSTRATED

Music and pictures of musicians are found in a very wide range of different types of manuscript. The illustrations for this book were taken from the following British Library manuscripts:–

Add. MS 12228. Helie de Borron, *Roman du Roi Meliadus de Leonnoys*. France, 1352–1362.

Add. MS 17302. Monastic Diurnal. Lyon, twelfth century.

Add. MS 19768. Troper and Proser. Mainz, second half of tenth century.

Add. MS 24680. Gradual. Weingarten, twelfth century.

Add. MS 27695. *Tractatus de septem vitiis*. Genoa, late fourteenth century.

Add. MS 27865. Sticherarion. Greece (Diocese of Joannina), thirteenth century.

Add. MS 28550. Fragmentary compilation volume. Robertsbridge, Sussex, *circa* 1325–50.

Add. MS 30014. Augustinian Hymnal. Siena, 1415.

Add. MS 30337. Exultet roll. Montecassino, *circa* 1072.

Add. MS 30845. Mozarabic Liber Misticus. Silos, tenth or early eleventh century.

Add. MS 32247. Part of a Gradual, bound with other texts. Tegernsee, Bavaria, end of eleventh century.

Add. MS 36881. Troper with polyphony. South of France, twelfth or early thirteenth century.

Add. MS 38122. Bible History in Flemish. Flanders, mid-fifteenth century.

Add. MS 42130. Psalter of Sir Geoffrey Luttrell. England, second quarter of fourteenth century.

Add. MS 47680. Pseudo-Aristotle, *De secretis secretorum*, copied by Walter de Milemete. England, 1326–7.

Add. MS 49622. Psalter. Gorleston, Norfolk, *circa* 1310–20.

Add. MS 57950. Choirbook. England, *circa* 1415–25.

Add. MS 62925. The Rutland Psalter. London or Salisbury, *circa* 1250–60.

Arundel MS 14. Giraldus Cambrensis, *Topographia Hiberniae*, with miscellaneous verses and later musical additions. England, thirteenth century (music fourteenth century).

Arundel MS 77. Musical treatises by Aurelian of Réôme, Boethius, Berno of Reichenau and the anonymous *Musica Enchiriadis*. Germany, end of eleventh century.

Arundel MS 83 I. Psalter and fragmentary Hours of the Passion (Howard Psalter). Norfolk (possibly St German's), *circa* 1310–20.

Cotton MS Caligula A XIV. Troper and Proser. England (possibly Winchester), late eleventh and twelfth centuries.

Cotton MS Tiberius A VII. Guillaume de Deguileville's *Pilgrimage of the Life of Man*, translated into Middle English verse by John Lydgate. Probably West Suffolk, *circa* 1430–1450.

Cotton MS Vespasian A I. Roman Psalter with Old English gloss. Probably Canterbury, second half of eighth century.

Cotton MS Vitellius A XIX. Bede, *Lives of St Cuthbert*, with verses and two musical additions. England, mid-tenth century.

Egerton MS 274. Trouvère songs. Northern France, thirteenth century.

Egerton MS 1070. Book of Hours of René of Anjou. France, mid-fifteenth century.

Egerton MS 2615. Circumcision Office and Play of Daniel. Beauvais, 1227–34.

Egerton MS 3307. Holy Week music and carols. Windsor or Meaux Abbey, 1430–44.

Harley MS 110. Works of Prosper and Isidore, with fragments of a Gradual used as flyleaves. Flyleaves probably Winchester, mid-eleventh century.

Harley MS 978. A miscellaneous anthology of music, medical texts and verse. Probably Reading, mid-thirteenth century.

Harley MS 1117. Verses on St Edward, Bede's *Lives of St Cuthbert*, Offices of Sts Cuthbert, Guthlac and Benedict. England (possibly Canterbury), early eleventh century.

Harley MS 2804. Bible. Worms, *circa* 1148.

Harley MS 2888. Psalter. England, 1340.

Harley MS 2917. Book of Hours. France, late fifteenth century.

Harley MS 3011. St Gregory, *Dialogues*. Possibly Liège, mid-eleventh century.

Harley MS 3095. Boethius, *De consolatione philosophiae* and other works. Rhineland, first half of tenth century.

Harley MS 4375. Valerius Maximus, *Dictorum et factorum memorabilium liber*. France, *circa* 1475.

Harley MS 4951. Gradual. Toulouse, eleventh century.

Harley MS 5237. Boethius, *De musica*. Unknown provenance, twelfth century.

Or. Add. MS 14761. Haggadah with piyyutim. Barcelona, mid-fourteenth century.

Or. Add. MS 18603. Sharaknotz (Hymnal). Armenia (probably Arbela), 1312.

Royal MS 2 B IV. Gradual and Troper. St Albans, second half of twelfth century.

Royal MS 6 E IX. Verse addressed to Robert of Anjou from the people of Prato. Prato, Tuscany, *circa* 1335–1340.

Royal MS 8 C XIII. Troper. Normandy, twelfth century.

Royal MS 15 D III. Bible history in French, based on Petrus Comestor's *Historia Scholastica*. France, early fifteenth century.

Sloane MS 3983. *Liber astrologiae*. Burgundy or Flanders, second half of fourteenth century.

Stowe MS 17. Book of Hours in Latin and French. Flanders (probably Maastricht), *circa* 1300.

Yates Thompson MS 8. Breviary of Renaud de Bar, Bishop of Metz. France, 1302–4.

Opposite: the angelic orchestra. Add. MS 30014, f. 124v.

INDEX

THE AUTHOR

Nicolas Bell is a curator of music manuscripts at the British Library. His doctoral thesis was a study of the Las Huelgas Codex, the most important Spanish source of polyphonic music of the thirteenth and fourteenth centuries. He is currently involved in a research project on liturgical poetry of the twelfth century.

Cover Illustration: Three clerics sing the motet 'Zelo tui langueo' from a roll. Arundel MS 83, f. 63v.

Half-title Page: Trumpeters with puffed-out cheeks. Royal MS 15 D III, f. 394.

Frontispiece: King David with lyre, surrounded by trumpters and dancers. Cotton MS Vespasian A I, f. 30v.

Title Page: King David as organist with bellows boy and hurdy-gurdy player. Add. MS 62925, f. 97v.

Illustration facing Introduction: Trumpets sound before the ark while a group of soft instruments play below. Harley MS 2917, f. 93.

First published 2001 by

The British Library

96 Euston Road

London NW1 2DB

British Library Cataloguing in Publication Data

A catalogue record for this book is available from The British Library

ISBN 0 7123 4706 2

Designed and typeset by Crayon Design, Stoke Row, Henley-on-Thames

Colour origination by Crayon Design and South Sea International Press

Printed in Hong Kong by South Sea International Press